enjoying
Cardinals
more

by Howard Youth

Contents

PHOTOS.COM

BILL THOMPSON, III (3)

Enjoying Cardinals More *was produced by the staff of*
Bird Watcher's Digest: *Bill Thompson, III, Booklet Editor
and Booklet Concept; Andy Thompson, Publisher, BWD Press;
Dawnrae Johanek, Editorial Consultant; Jim Cirigliano, Managing
Editor; Claire Mullen, Production Director.*

Bird Watcher's Digest *is published by Pardson Corporation,
P.O. Box 110, Marietta, OH 45750. To order additional copies
of* Enjoying Cardinals More, *or our other booklets,* Enjoying
Hummingbirds More, The Backyard Bird Watcher's Answer
Guide, Creating Your Backyard Bird Garden, Enjoying Squir-
rels More (or Less), Understanding Bats, Creating Your Water
Garden, Enjoying Butterflies More, Enjoying Bird Feeding More,
Enjoying Purple Martins More, Enjoying Bluebirds More, Enjoy-
ing Woodpeckers More, An ID Guide to Backyard Birds, *and* A
Guide to Bird Homes, *or for BWD subscription information, call
toll-free at 1-800-879-2473 or visit birdwatchersdigest.com on
the Internet.*

BIRD WATCHER'S *Digest*

Introduction:

Red, Fed, Much More to Be Said

If you are lucky enough to live in cardinal country, you likely see them all the time. At the feeders, they flock to sunflower seed offerings. They flit from trees and bushes at the parking lot edge. They pop up in most wooded birding spots. Who does not delight at the loud chip, or the flashing red of a male on snow?

Northern cardinals are charismatic, adaptable, and, luckily for us, abundant over much of their extensive range. It's hard to imagine a more colorful creature to grace our dooryards. Perhaps that's why the cardinal is emblazoned on baseball hats and football helmets, and why it was chosen as the state bird in seven states: Illinois, Indiana, Kentucky, North Carolina, Ohio, Virginia, and West Virginia. According to data compiled by the Cornell Lab of Ornithology and collected from thousands of backyard birders, the northern cardinal was the most frequently reported bird in the South, at 97 percent of reporting backyards. In the Mid-Atlantic states, the cardinal ranked seventh, and in central states it was number eight. If you have these shocking red songbirds in your neighborhood, you are likely to see them year-round. They will stick it out, hot summers or cold winters. You can't pick your neighbors, it's true; but with a cheery bird like the cardinal, you may be happy with at least one that you've got!

Earth is blessed with about 10,000 bird species. North America has a generous batch of colorful fowl, and the cardinal certainly ranks high on the "eye candy" list, alongside tanagers, buntings, hummingbirds, and others. But for all their brilliance and in-your-face abundance, even cardinals have their secrets. There's simply so much that is not known about these songbirds, and so much that biologists and birders alike are learning about them.

So, pull up a chair and let's explore the world of the cardinal. You'll soon see that your backyard birds are doing things you never realized until you had the chance to learn more about them. And we'll discover the answers to questions many people have about the northern cardinal.

BILL THOMPSON, III

The male northern cardinal is our only all-red crested bird.

A Common Backyard Visitor
What *is* a Cardinal?

A cardinal is a high-ranking member of the Roman Catholic Church. A cardinal is also a bird. No mere coincidence here. The bird was named after the clergy member's ceremonial scarlet robes and high, pointed hat. The rose-red plumage of the male cardinal and the crests of adult cardinals make them a near-perfect match for this name. The scientific name *Cardinalis cardinalis* makes the point twice.

Actually, there are many common names for this familiar bird. They include Virginia redbird, common cardinal, cardinal grosbeak, and Virginia nightingale. But the familiar "redbird" or cardinal is most correctly called the **northern cardinal**, for reasons you'll read here. Taxonomists—scientists who categorize birds and other wildlife into specific species, then groups of species called genera (plural of genus), then groups of genera called families—place the northern cardinal in the three-species songbird genus *Cardinalis*. It shares this genus with the **pyrrhuloxia** (*Cardinalis sinuatus*) of the Southwest and Mexico and the **vermilion cardinal** (*Cardinalis phoeniceus*), which lives in thorny scrub and cactus thickets along the Caribbean coasts of Venezuela and Colombia. The vermilion cardinal is a longer-crested bird but is very similar in appearance. The male's overall coloration, however, is a closer match to the more pinkish-red summer tanager. Also, it lacks the wide black mask. Instead of red-orange, its bill is pale bluish gray.

At first glance, the pyrrhuloxia looks like a long-crested, bent-billed female cardinal. Many folks in the West call it the desert cardinal. But instead of black rimming the face and throat, the male has red, which runs from chin to vent. There's red on its tail and wings too, but otherwise, the male's coloration is gray. The female has a pale yellowish bill and less rich but similar coloration to a female cardinal. Unlike the more or less straight-edge bill of the cardinal, the pyrrhuloxia has a curved, but also thick bill. It's interesting to watch northern cardinals and pyrrhuloxias feeding or singing side by side where they share habitat, from south Texas to southeastern Arizona and south into Mexico. There, individuals of the two species stake out territories (singing similar songs), feed, and raise their young side by side, apparently without com-

Male northern cardinal (left) confronting a male pyrrhuloxia, a closely related species.

peting with each other.

The genus *Cardinalis* is one of a dozen in the family Cardinalidae, yet another name that celebrates the famed red bird. Family members include the grosbeaks, including North America's rose-breasted, black-headed, and blue grosbeaks; the colorful buntings, including indigo, lazuli, and painted; the dickcissel; and the saltators, which are thick-billed and somewhat sparrow-like tropical songbirds.

If you visit Hawaii, you may see cardinals there. They are not native, but are among the many colorful species released and naturalized there. Among the other songbirds you may see in Hawaii—or in their native South America—are the red-crested cardinal and yellow-billed cardinal. These South American birds, while superficially similar in appearance to our cardinal, belong to a different family, Emberizidae, which includes the Old World buntings, sparrows, towhees, seedeaters, and a few South American birds commonly called cardinals—yellow, red-cowled, red-capped, and crimson-fronted.

So, there are human cardinals, birds called cardinals in common name only, cardinals in the cardinal genus, but only one bird—the northern cardinal or *Cardinalis cardinalis*—that's a cardinal through and through.

Watching
Cardinal Behavior

Back around 1980, I took a snapshot of my parent's backyard with my simple Brownie camera. You can see the hopper feeder I got as a birthday gift, adorned with a few dark round spots, perhaps sparrows or finches. But I remember being pleased that the photo showed one bird you could easily identify. There, below the feeder, a bright red spot in the snow—a northern cardinal. Thirty years later, I still delight at the unbelievable delicious apple-red of a male cardinal glowing in the snow. And I still marvel at how lucky we are to have this bright bird, which would, with a little imagination, fit perfectly in a tropical setting. Yet there they are in our backyards, not in the Amazon, sticking it out with us all year long.

Like the bright red of a stop-light, though, familiarity can lull us into overlooking the cardinal and its fascinating behaviors. Before you glance out back and think, "Oh, it's just another cardinal," keep in mind that the more you watch, the more you are likely to see. Cardinals' lives are not simple and neatly programmed. A cardinal's life is full of activities and sudden circumstances that require immediate response. Cardinals and other birds must

be adaptable to survive, and they must be tough. Behaviors change day to day, and vary between individuals or from season to season. Watch cardinals with this in mind, and you may find yourself with more questions than answers.

Just look at the social lives of cardinals, for example. You may often see cardinals in pairs. But outside the breeding season you may find dozens of cardinals beneath your feeders. Such feeding frenzies often take place around dawn and dusk, when cardinal colors don't stand out as much in the snow. This is helpful timing when sharp-shinned or Cooper's hawks—bird-eating predators—are around. But in difficult weather, a large number of cardinals may show up any time during the day.

While cardinal pairs often stay together, it doesn't mean that cardinals are always what human beings would call "faithful." In the world of birds, a couple may stay together at breeding and nesting time, but the father of the young is not always the one defending the territory or helping feed the young. Genetic studies of cardinals revealed that between nine and 35 percent of young result from a female mating with a male other than her assumed mate.

Enjoying Cardinals More

After bathing, this young female northern cardinal takes a drink.

The cardinal "courtship kiss" involves a male presenting a bit of food to a female.

Males stay close to females throughout breeding season, perhaps in part to ensure their paternity. Early observers took this more as a strictly protective measure. In the late 1800s, famed nature writer and inveterate cardinal fan Olive Thorne Miller wrote: "As the head of a family the cardinal is admirable, not only in his attentions to his lovely dove-colored mate, but in singing to her by the hour, and in protecting her from intrusion or danger."

In their day-to-day movements, cardinals use natural cover that's available to them but are not so skulking that a birder can't quickly identify them. When feeding on the ground, cardinals hop. Their flight from perch to perch is undulating, and provides the observer ample opportunities to see them spread and flash their colorful wings and tails.

A steadily warming climate and the explosive growth of bird-feeding as a hobby over the last 30 or 40 years likely helped cardinals move into areas once assumed to be far too snowy and cold for them. The birds can withstand intense winter chills, fluffing their feathers and nestling bills into scapulars (shoulder feathers) while at rest. Fluffing traps air between feathers and body, boosting insulation. During periods of intense cold, cardinals also increase their metabolic rate while reducing their water loss.

But the hardy cardinal has its limits. These pioneering birds have not pushed much past Canada's southeastern fringe. Beyond this point, relatively few songbirds brave the winters. These include some members of the crow clan, some chickadees, red-breasted nuthatches, redpolls, crossbills, pine and evening grosbeaks, and pine siskins.

Across the East, early signs of spring include the appearance of skunk cabbage, the return of phoebes to the north, the peenting of woodcocks—and cardinal courtship displays, which start occurring as early as late January or February, even in southern Canada.

Pairing Up, Flocking, Divorcing

Scientists still puzzle over when and why cardinal pairs join or part ways. Some pairs stay on their territory through the year. Many do not. Many join large winter feeding flocks. But pairs form not only during nesting seasons but also in fall. Scientists have chronicled "divorces" among cardinals during different times of the year, when mates leave mates and find new ones. This is perhaps regular but probably not frequent. Many of the pairs you see at your feeders are likely formed pairs that will carry over to the next mating season. But if one mate dies, the other will go on, eventually finding another mate.

Cardinals also surprise many birders when they see females sing. This usually takes place in spring. The female's song is generally not as forceful and has a sweeter tone.

Cardinal pairs frequently win the admiration of their human observers. After pairs bond and begin staking out nest sites within their territories, there's a lot of close behavior going on. Pairs bond or maintain their bonds through courtship displays. At the early stages of their "relationship" a male will twist and turn toward a female, showing his breast, spreading his wings, while he lowers his crest and flattens his feathers. Males also sing while swaying back and forth, and perform a fluttering song flight toward their mates.

As things progress, males feed the females, who shake their wings and act as though they are begging for food. When ready to mate, a female will raise her head and tail, lower her wings, and fluff her feathers.

A pair works together to select the nest site. A female will fluff and turn, then fly off, followed by her mate. As the mates call to each other, they pick up potential nesting materials. If a predator intrudes upon the nest area, a cardinal pair will often work with other birds to mob it until it leaves.

Cardinals can also be not-so-nice to each other. I'm referring here to territorial disputes that flare up before and during the breeding season. You may also see cardinals squabble over feeding space at or beneath your feeders or at a bird bath. Cardinals may lunge but they rarely fight with each other. Instead, a bird may lower its crest and call *Kee-too* or *chuck* and even shake its wings and lunge forward. During breeding season, males will relentlessly chase other males away from the nest area and females will chase off other females. Both males and females, however, will sneak off their territory from time to time. And they may at times return "home" after mating with another cardinal that is not their "true" mate.

Territorial fighting stops by late summer. Some time around the onset of fall, you will notice that you are not just seeing cardinal pairs or their young. Feeding flocks start forming. These fluid groups of birds likely start as parents traveling around with some of their young. Some cardinals, however, may stay on territory much or all of the year. But generally cardinal pairs spend the "off season" drifting in and out of feeding flocks that ebb and flow as local pairs or small groups come and go. It's not unusual for backyard birders to see dawn or dusk assemblages of 20 or more cardinals. In West Virginia, flocks of up to 100 have been reported. Flock sizes likely vary by weather, habitat, time of day, and time of year.

Winter feeding flocks often contain roughly equal numbers of males and females. Flocks loosely associate with sparrows, juncos, goldfinches, towhees, and other songbirds. They all benefit from safety in numbers, especially in winter months, when deciduous trees and shrubs are bare, giving predators clearer sight lines.

If you're lucky, you may catch sight of cardinals partaking in one of the more bizarre bird behaviors: anting. For more than 60 years, ornithologists have chronicled birds either rubbing ants over wing and tail feathers or simply letting ants swarm over them. Yet few agree on exactly why cardinals and other birds ant. There are hypotheses, though: Perhaps the formic acid exuded by the insects helps birds repel lice and other parasites, or perhaps it protects them from infection. Or maybe the acid tingles and soothes skin irritation during molting. Or anting might remove unpalatable substances, such as formic acid, from ants so the cardinals can eat them. This remains just one area of cardinal natural history that begs for more investigation. Other mysteries remain, including the details on how extreme temperatures may stress eggs, how often incubating females leave the nest, how fast fledglings grow and reach adult size, as well as more details on the

CHARLES W. MELTON

Cardinals relish a good splashing soak in a bird bath.

lives of immature birds.

While you have learned about a wide variety of cardinal behaviors, like any creature, some cardinals don't exactly fit the mold and behave exactly as described. In the 1950s, for example, a male cardinal fed goldfish in a North Carolina backyard pond day after day (perhaps it had lost its own young?). And cardinals have also occasionally fed the young of other bird species.

A cardinal's life is full of dangers: harsh weather, predators, competitors, parasites and illnesses. Many do not live to a ripe old age. But some do. Despite all the threats, at least one wild cardinal lived almost 16 years. A captive bird allegedly held on for 28 and a half years.

At the Nest

Many times, cardinals nest almost right under our noses. Sure, they are out in the open about singing and their loud chips are easy to detect. But they get stealthy when it comes to nests and eggs, hiding them in dense foliage. But that foliage might include the unruly forsythia hedge out back, or perhaps that fast-growing honeysuckle alongside the house. Careful, patient observation will lead you to cardinal nests, revealing a rich trove of avian secrets that will broaden your knowledge of these colorful birds and enhance your appreciation of them. Cardinal territories range in size from a half acre to six and a half acres. If you live in a typical suburban area, you may share a cardinal territory

JULIE ZICKEFOOSE

A fledgling northern cardinal.

Start your cardinal nest search by surveying your property or neighborhood for small trees, shrubs, and vines. Honeysuckle, multiflora rose, and blackberry shrubs could be candidates for a nest search, especially those draped in wild grape or other vines. But cardinals nest in a wide variety of trees and shrubs. Just a few others: hawthorn, dogwood, red cedar, white spruce, pines, hemlocks, arborvitae, elm, maples, black locust, box elder, and elderberry.

Notice a singing male's proximity to these features. Territorial males usually sing from exposed perches, and they will periodically chase off other males. Males and females will attack windows and rear-view mirrors that show their antagonistic reflections. If a nest contains young, he will be spending a lot of time delivering food to his mate and young.

A cardinal pair's first clutch of eggs is usually laid from around the third week in March, which is considered early, to some time in early to mid-April. Throughout nesting season, though, if you catch sight of a female, watch her with particular care. Females usually build the nest alone, although the male will bring her food and perhaps a few construction materials. The nest-building process takes as little as three to nine days or, especially in the case of the first nest of the season, as long as two to three weeks. The

with your neighbors. Or you may live at the intersection of two territories.

Cardinals spend the better part of spring and summer nesting. They generally raise two to three broods a season, but often after several attempts fail when predators snap up eggs or young. Other threats include marauding cowbirds, freak weather, and perhaps untimely encounters when pruning gear meets nesting branch. Multiple nesting attempts keep cardinal pairs busy. That makes for good cardinal watching. From late January almost through August—seven months—there is some kind of breeding-relating activity going on, from territorial squabbles to courtship, nest-building to incubation. Then the raising of young.

C-3
5

8257

0006943

00069438257

**Sell your books at
sellbackyourBook.com!**
Go to sellbackyourBook.com
and get an instant price quote.
We even pay the shipping - see
what your old books are worth
today!

female snaps twigs with her strong bill and turns in the nest, tamping down materials with her feet.

With all the comings and goings, a diligent observer is bound to get strong clues as to where the nest is hidden. Fortunately for us, cardinals rarely place their nests higher than ten feet, so you should be able to get a good view once you find the nest. Look as low as three feet above the ground in low shrubs as well as up in tallish small trees. And remember that cardinals favor vines tangled between their trees and bushes. Such green screening enables them to nest alongside our homes without being detected. If you do find a cardinal nest, observe it from a distance, through your binoculars. While your scent on or near the nest will not cause the adult cardinals any concern, it may serve as a pointer for a predator following in your footsteps.

If the parents are absent, how can you identify a cardinal nest? Well, you can start by learning what a cardinal nest and eggs look like, even if they resemble those of other songbirds. The open cup nest is usually wedged between thin branches and is made up of organic materials including weeds, thin twigs, grasses, strips of bark, leaves, and tiny roots. The inside of the nest, the soft lining upon which the eggs rest, is lined with thin grasses or soft hair. Cardinals, however, do get a bit trashy: They often festoon the outer cup of the nest with paper or plastic strips.

Between a day and a week after she finishes the nest, the female lays on average two to three eggs, which she incubates for 11 or 12 days. She does not lay all eggs at once, however: Generally, she lays one a day for two or three days. During incubation, the male brings the female food.

Cardinal eggs are somewhat glossy and whitish or greenish white with streaks and splotches of chocolate brown, purplish or gray. These marks are usually found all over the egg, but may be more widely distributed at the broader end. Cowbird eggs, which are often laid in cardinal nests, are smaller, often with finer markings.

Once hatched, young cardinals remain in the nest for nine

JULIE ZICKEFOOSE

Cardinal nests are often well concealed in thick cover in a tree or bush.

Both parents feed the fledglings for several weeks after they leave the nest.

feel that they are in jeopardy, contact a licensed animal rehabilitator. It is unlawful to take in wild birds without a license.

Once out of the nest, young cardinals need about a week more before they truly earn their wings and become strong flyers. In fact, fledged cardinals usually stick very close to the nest, not venturing far from their perches during their first week of "freedom." And fledglings still receive most of their food from their parents for two to three weeks more. Males will take on more feeding as females settle in to start the next brood at a new nest (cardinals rarely reuse their nests). Whether fed by one or both parents, young cardinals generally do not go totally out on their own until between 25 and 55 days after they have left their nest. The tables turn for them the following year: Young cardinals usually start breeding the spring that follows their hatching.

to 11 days, while both parents scramble to keep them well fed, stuffing a wide variety of insects, spiders, and other small invertebrates down their yellow-fringed, bright red-orange gullets. When it comes to house-cleaning, there's no fuss or muss for the busy parents: They simply snap up the nestlings' waste, which is packaged in a tight white parcel called a fecal sac, and either eat it (early on) or flap away with it, dropping it far from the nest.

If you find a nest and know there are young inside, and if the young beg loud enough for you to easily hear them, give the nest a wide berth. Nestlings have strong voices by the fifth day, and by the eighth day disturbance could cause them to fledge, or leave the nest, prematurely. Fully feathered young cardinals that tumble out of their nests early will be found and fed by attending parents. They usually do not need to be rescued. If for some reason you

As you have read, cardinal nests often fail. Chalk up the birds' abundance, at least in part, to sheer persistence. It also explains why you may notice cardinals with fledged young while the female next door might still be sitting on eggs. You may even see young cardinals just out of the nest in late August or even early September, when migratory species such as orioles have already begun their southbound journeys. ✒

Vital Statistics

Northern Cardinal (*cardinalis cardinalis*)

Length: 8 ½ to 9 inches (21.59 to 22.86 cm)

Wingspan: 10 to 12 inches (25.4 to 30.48 cm)

Weight: Around 1.5 ounces

Eggs: Usually two or three. Somewhat glossy, whitish or greenish white with chocolate brown, purplish or gray streaks and splotches.

Diet: Seeds, berries, buds, flowers, insects, spiders, and other small invertebrates.

BILL THOMPSON, III

Female cardinals show only patches of red in adult plumage.

Showing Their True Colors

In all plumages, free-flying cardinals show at least some red:

Males are *all* red, except for their thick red-orange bills and broad black mask and throat.

Females have red crests, wings, and tails. Red shows both on their upper and under wings as they fly. They too have black framing their red-orange bills. Otherwise, they are a rich fawn brown, somewhat yellowish below and somewhat darker on the back.

Juveniles have warm buffy tones like females, and reddish on wings and tail. But they lack the black around bill and throat and their bills are lead-gray until they reach about two months to 80 days after hatching.

Cardinals

Male cardinals brighten even the most dreary winter day.

MASLOWSKI PRODUCTIONS

In most areas, cardinals stay around all year. But that doesn't mean that they are up to the same business all year. Nor do all cardinals stay put. Here's a look at the cardinal year:

Winter
Feeding flocks, particularly at dawn and dusk, visit feeders and brushy edge habitat. Beginning from late January into March, males and females begin defending territories.

Spring
Pair bonds, territory, nest-building, incubation, young, feeding, first fledged young.

Summer
Through at least two-thirds of summer: pair bonds, territory, nest-building, incubation, young, feeding, fledged young up until late summer. Territorial disputes drop off by late summer.

Fall
Territories no longer defended. Pair bonds can still be formed. Feeding flocks form.

ROBERTMCCAW.COM

Cardinals can raise
or lower their
head crests.

Habitat
Where They Live

Northern cardinals live in tree- and bush-rich habitats virtually throughout the eastern United States and also, locally, in the Southwest (particularly the southern half of Arizona) and Mexico, south to northern Guatemala and Belize. In Mexico, cardinals are found through the eastern part of the country, including the entire Yucatan Peninsula, in southern Baja California, and in parts of the northwest and the southern Pacific Coast. In the East, outside the frigid northern extremes of their range, they are common and one of the more familiar visitors to backyard bird feeders.

Eighteen cardinal subspecies have been described. In the field, however, birders will be unable to distinguish the subtle differences between most. These include slight differences in bills; crests; wing, tail, and feet length; markings; and coloration.

The most noticeable dif-

Any kind of brushy habitat can be home to cardinals within their mostly eastern range.

Enjoying Cardinals More

Northern Cardinal
(*Cardinalis cardinalis*)
Range Map

☐ Year-round range

ferences can be seen between eastern and southwestern subspecies: Southwestern males have longer crests, less extensive black over the top of the bill, and an overall paler coloration. The bill is larger too, with a more curved culmen, or middle edge of the mandibles.

More than a century ago, cardinals were considered eastern birds found only as far north as southern New England and southern New York. These days, backyard birders find them throughout New York and as far north as the southern fringes of Nova Scotia, New Brunswick, Quebec, Ontario, and through most of eastern Maine.

Cardinals are considered non-migratory. In other words,

throughout their range they are permanent residents. Young birds, however, disperse to find new territories. They have likely been the pioneers that forged new inroads as the species has expanded its range.

The cardinal's northbound march may have been due to a combination of factors, including warmer climate, winter feeding stations stocked with sunflower seeds, and ever-expanding human settlements that create the kind of habitats they favor.

Unlike many declining bird species, northern cardinals thrive in human-developed areas, where there are not only feeders but also abundant plantings and reliable water

Sunflower seed, suet dough, mealworms, and fruit are among the foods cardinals eat at bird feeders.

sources. They occur in suburban and even some urban backyards, in parks, and also in wilder habitats. These include thickets, hedgerows, shrubby open areas including forest clearings, at the woodland's edge, in open woodlands, in bush-dotted grasslands, and in the shrubby fringes at the edge of wetlands. In the desert Southwest and Mexico, their red plumage flashes in lush riparian (river's edge) habitats, brambles, and desert washes. Throughout their range, northern cardinals can be found along fences, where vegetation sprouts up and is not regularly cleared. This could include blackberry tangles in the East or mesquite stands in the Southwest and Mexico.

Cardinals nest and hide in dense tangles of vegetation, often in small trees or bushes. They sing from prominent perches, which include branches, power lines, and roof tops. Recent studies have found that increased carbon dioxide levels in cities favor faster vine growth, a trend that would further enhance cardinal nesting choices.

As mentioned earlier, northern cardinals have been introduced to the Hawaiian Islands. First released in the 1920s or 1930s, they are now common on all of the main islands, although not as abundant as introduced house finches and Japanese white-eyes. Cardinals also found their way, via humans, to the island of Bermuda and around Los Angeles, California.

In winter, cardinals form large, loose flocks.

Cardinal
Songs & Sounds

"He is famous as a singer," wrote Olive Thorne Miller in 1901, "and is therefore trapped and caught in great numbers for cages. In Europe, where he is a favorite cage-bird, he is thought by many to be equal to the famous nightingale as a singer."

Cardinals are still kept as cage birds in Mexico, but today in the United States they are protected by law from harassment or capture. Wrote Miller: "The female cardinal is herself a charming singer, more pleasing to many than her mate, her music being softer in tone and otherwise different from his."

The cardinal's song is rich, loud, and easy to memorize: *Chewa-CHEER, Chewa-CHEER, Chewa-CHEER, WIT, WIT, WIT,* *WIT, WIT, WIT.* Or, another version goes: *WIT WIT WIT, CHEER, CHEER, CHEER, CHEER, CHEER.* Song dialects have been identified in different regions. In any part of cardinal country, one of these rich, cheery songs is bound to be among the most prominent components of an early dawn chorus on a spring or summer day.

The cardinal's strong *chip* note is also easily separated from the softer *chips* made by many warblers, juncos, and other songbirds. Cardinals chip when they are near each other and approaching roost sites, but they also have other calls. A higher *Kee-too* call and a *chuck* note can be heard when a bird is agitated, such as when two males square off at the edge of territories.

Male cardinals sing frequently — even on sunny winter days.

Male cardinals usually sing from a prominent perch.

Predators to
Parasites to Pathogens

Cardinals cannot easily escape attention from predators. Pairs may lose so many eggs or young that they might attempt to nest up to eight times in a season. Rarely do they succeed in raising a full brood more than two or three times per year. According to a study of 121 Ohio cardinal nests that was published in the journal *The Condor* in 1994, "a high incidence of predation by a rich guild of nest predators precludes the existence of predictably safe nest sites for cardinals. Instead, cardinals simply appear to be well-adapted to re-nest rapidly in response to the near randomness of nest predation."

Cardinal eggs and young end up on the menu for a variety of predators. Milk snakes, black racers, and other snakes slither into nests and devour them. Among avian attackers are crows and blue jays, which eat eggs and young, and house wrens, which puncture cardinal eggs that they find within their territories. Brown-headed, and in the Southwest and Mexico, bronzed cowbirds sometimes remove and even eat cardinal eggs when they slink onto nests to lay their eggs there. Fox squirrels, red squirrels, and eastern chipmunks have been seen eating eggs.

Meanwhile, adults and juveniles fall prey to accipiters, especially Cooper's and sharp-shinned hawks, as well as domestic cats and dogs. Shrikes kill cardinals from time to time as well, as do eastern gray squirrels on rare occasion. Owls, including screech and long-eared, grab them from their roosting sites by night.

Cardinals have a longer breeding season than do cowbirds. Even where cowbird parasitism occurs at high rates it usually happens early in the season. This may be because many other hosts become available as nesting season progresses, including Neotropical migrants such as warblers. But even when cowbird young are present in cardinal nests, cardinals frequently raise their young alongside the interlopers. In fact, studies indicate that cowbird young don't have great success in cardinal nests because many nests are preyed upon and because when cardinal eggs hatch before those of cowbirds, the cowbirds do not fare as well as the cardinals.

Like other birds, cardinals play host to bird-specific parasites including ticks, mites, and lice. These last two *may* be one of the reasons bald-headed cardinals are sometimes seen (see "Frequently Asked Questions" at the end of the booklet).

Enjoying Cardinals More

Hopper feeders are very attractive to cardinals.

Like all animals, cardinals can get sick. You can help keep them healthy by washing your feeders and bird baths—year-round—at least once a month with a light bleach solution that is nine parts water to one part bleach. After cleaning, rinse thoroughly and allow to air dry before you refill.

Also, regularly rake away old seed husks and droppings from beneath your feeders. These build up and can contain pathogens. While cardinals perch on hopper-type feeders, they spend much of their time foraging on the ground.

Fortunately, recent studies indicate that cardinals are not severely impacted by West Nile Virus, an introduced disease that has spread across the country since appearing in New York in 1999. Among the songbird species hard hit by this mosquito-transmitted disease: American crows, blue jays, tufted titmice, house wrens, American robins, and bluebirds.

Also, cardinals, at least for now, do not seem very susceptible to conjunctivitis caused by the bacterium *Mycoplasma gallisepticum*. This ailment, now widespread among house finch populations, is tagged as a culprit in sharp declines in that species in the East.

Attracting Cardinals: Food, Water, and Backyard Habitat

Food and Water

The single most attractive feeder food for cardinals is black-oil sunflower seed. They also readily eat striped sunflower. For the bird feeding gourmet, higher-priced sunflower chips, sunflower hearts, and safflower seed are readily accepted cardinal treats. But cardinals also eat millet, cracked corn, and small fruits.

Which types of feeders do cardinals favor? Well, they can't hang upside-down or cling nimbly to a tiny perch like a chickadee, titmouse, goldfinch, or nuthatch. But standard hopper feeders and wide-open platform feeders are great for them. Also, they'll perch on a seed tray if one is attached to the bottom of a tube feeder. And cardinals feed on the ground as well.

Over a year, a cardinal's diet includes about 70 percent plant matter and about 30 percent animal matter. But if you look season by season, the picture changes. Of course, in northern winters, almost all food will be from plants.

Cardinals will snap up mealworms offered in a tall-sided feeder with a rain-protecting roof. This protein source may be particularly useful to cardinals while they are raising their young in spring and summer. Young cardinals are fed almost exclusively insects and other invertebrates.

But you can also provide more "natural" foods by planting trees that provide cardinals nourishment. Cardinals eat tree buds and flower buds and blooms in spring, and berries throughout the year. They will take ripe berries from hollies, sumacs, cherries, mulberries, dogwoods, and hackberry, among many others. Dense shrubs and small trees conceal nests and provide shelter.

Like other birds, cardinals require safe, clean sources of water for drinking and bathing. Bird baths should be emptied and refilled daily if possible. Also, feeders and bird baths should be cleaned using a bleach solution of nine parts water to one part bleach at least once a month. Rinse well and allow to air dry before refilling.

A small backyard water feature with moving water, such as a small pond with re-circulating pump and filter, will draw cardinals and other birds close to your home. Make sure the vegetation around the pond is not too dense, so as not to shield a cat seeking easy pickings at the water's edge.

Enjoying Cardinals More

Cardinals will visit
tube feeders but
prefer to use hoppper
or platform feeders
for easier access to seed.

In spring and summer, cardinal pairs are often seen together.

Backyard Habitat

As you prune, clean up, and plant in your yard, keep cardinals in mind. You can attract cardinals to nest by planting or maintaining trees and shrubs and, where possible, fostering tangles of vegetation.

Not all vines are desirable for you and your habitat, however. Some vines are invasive and can take over and even kill trees and shrubs. These include fast-growing, introduced vines such as porcelainberry, kudzu, oriental bittersweet, Asiatic wisteria, and English ivy.

Poison ivy is native. Although its berries are relished by birds, the plant is a nuisance or danger to most humans. Most people given some contact with it have some type of allergic reaction to poison ivy. Greenbrier, Virginia creeper, and native wisteria are among the easily controlled native vines.

Another backyard habitat element is the brush pile. Fashioned from loosely arranged dead branches and other yard brush, this heap provides added shelter for your cardinals, wrens, sparrows, and other wildlife. If you have room in your backyard, you can "plant" tall dead tree limbs in the ground. These bare snags provide look-out and singing perches for cardinals and other birds.

The cardinals' thick bill provides the cutting and crushing power needed to extract the soft seeds from their protective husks. Among the plants that cardinals feed upon are wild grapes, blackberry, dogwood and mulberries, various grasses, sedges, hackberry, and knotweed. They may also be busy scouring your trees and lawn edge for beetles, crickets, grasshoppers, katydids, cicadas, leafhoppers, caterpillars, moths, true bugs, flies, spiders, centipedes, snails, and other invertebrates.

Enjoying Cardinals More

Your home is part of your habitat. While cardinals will not be living in your house, they may bash into it unless you take steps to break up reflections on large windows. Window strikes kill many feeder birds around homes when they fly into reflective glass at top speeds, mistaking them for trees mirrored in them. There are a few steps you can take to try to minimize such often-fatal encounters:

1 Attach static-adhering or regular stickers to your large windows.

2 Hang or arrange broken branches by the glass.

3 Hang tinsel, strips of Mylar, used CDs, aluminum foil pie pans, or other shiny, noticeable objects to deter birds.

4 Move your feeder close to your house so hawk-flushed birds will see your window before hitting it; if they do collide, the closer strike may be less damaging.

5 You could tape up falcon or owl silhouettes, but these pictures may only serve to break up reflections rather than scare the birds away from windows.

Do your own experimenting after checking out the situation outside, from the cardinal's perspective, at different times of day. ➤

Cardinals, like other birds, are sometimes victims of window strikes.

Tips and Tricks

Cardinal Rules

BILL THOMPSON, III (5)

Get a bit messy.

A wild, tangled area in the backyard that combines some vines, bushes, and small trees is a cardinal magnet.

Clean up your act.

Make sure you keep feeders and bird baths clean.

Keep your eye on the birdie.

Keep an eye on your cardinals to see different behaviors through the year.

Consider yourself lucky if you have northern cardinals. They only live in North America.

MASLOWSKI PRODUCTIONS

Break up reflections.

Address reflective glass issues by taking steps to break up window reflections that might cause window strikes.

Give the "all clear" signal.

Cats in, cardinals out. Keep Tabby indoors.

Welcome hawks.

Let the cardinals beware!

Frequently Asked
Questions

Q: How does a cardinal get its flashy red coloration?

A: Like flamingoes, cardinals get a good bit of their coloration from their diet. Fruits and seeds provide the carotenoid pigments cardinals need to give them their red coloration, and the birds eat many of these foods as they approach their fall molt. Sunflower and other seeds, on the other hand, are not good sources of these pigments.

Q: I've found a bald-headed cardinal in my backyard. What's up with that?

A: You're *not* seeing the result of a mating between a vulture and a cardinal here. From time to time, a strange-looking cardinal pops up, mainly during summer or fall. Its head may lack all of its head feathers or many of them. The cause of this baldness is but one of the cardinal mysteries that begs further study. Some cases may be caused by injury or parasites such as mites or lice. Many experts, however, believe that bald cardinals are molting, but instead of gradually replacing old feathers with new, for some reason most or all head feath-

ers fall off at once. For cardinals, summer and fall are normal molting times. The birds' head feathers are usually replaced within a few weeks.

Q: How can I get that crazy cardinal to stop attacking its reflection in my house window or car rear-view mirror?

A: Both male and female cardinals will attack their reflections, mistaking them for same-gender territorial rivals. If your rearview mirror is plagued, devise a cover for it. A car tarp or new, shaded parking spot may spare your car from the onslaught and steady stream of droppings that accompany such clashes. As for house windows that become a cardinal's "enemy," streamers or some kind of covering may help. Some homeowners have placed rubber snakes (from the toy store) by the affected windows. Or you could just put up with it, although it may keep up most of breeding season and continue the following year or more.

Q: A hawk killed a cardinal in my backyard. How do I get rid of the hawks and keep my cardinals safe? And what can I do to get rid of cats?